THE ART OF DRAWING AND CREATING
MANGA
MECHAS AND
MONSTERS

Books are to be ret

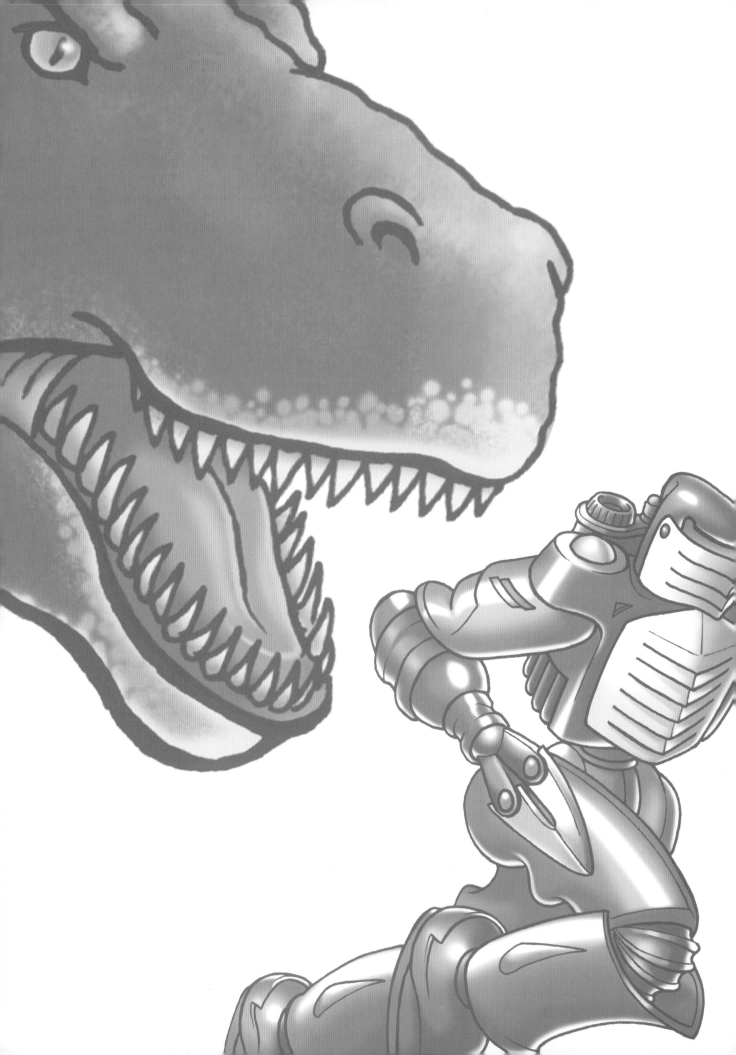

THE ART OF DRAWING AND CREATING

MANGA

MECHAS AND MONSTERS

PETER GRAY

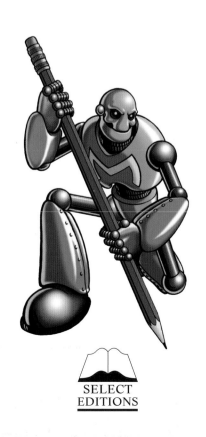

SELECT
EDITIONS

This edition printed in 2005

Selectabook Ltd
Folly Road, Roundway, Devizes,
Wiltshire SN10 2HT

Copyright © 2004, Arcturus Publishing Limited/Peter Gray
26/27 Bickels Yard, 151–153 Bermondsey Street,
London SE1 3HA

ISBN 1-84193-276-0

Artwork by Peter Gray
Cover and book design by Steve Flight
Digital colouring by David Stevenson

Printed in China

CONTENTS

NTROD

Although the main characters of manga comics and animes (the Japanese word for animations) are usually human, they are often supported by a cast of animals, robots, and monsters—from cuddly little four-legged sidekicks to enormous dinosaurs, robotic killing machines, and strange alien beasts. It's these weird and wonderful creatures that we'll be focusing on in this book. In many ways, they are the most interesting and enjoyable manga characters to draw.

Many of them—good and bad—are based in some way on men, women, and children, so you'll need to know how to draw human beings and, most importantly, how to adapt their features.

Manga now features in a huge range of magazines, computer games, and graphic novels. It is one of the most visible drawing styles in the world today, and one of the most popular among comic-book fans.

In *Mechas and Monsters* you'll find a wealth of exercises to get you started with drawing in the style. There are easy-to-follow steps for you to create a range of characters, and you'll also find plenty of examples to help you develop your own cast of amazing beings.

Don't be put off by the slick look of the artwork produced by professional artists—it isn't that hard to emulate once you know some of the tricks of the trade. Nor do you need to own a computer to produce interesting color work.

The most important skill for any aspiring manga artist to develop is the ability to draw, and this will only come about if you keep practicing. Don't limit yourself to just drawing in the manga style—try a range of different approaches. All this effort will pay off eventually, and you will notice how much more inventive and interesting your drawings become.

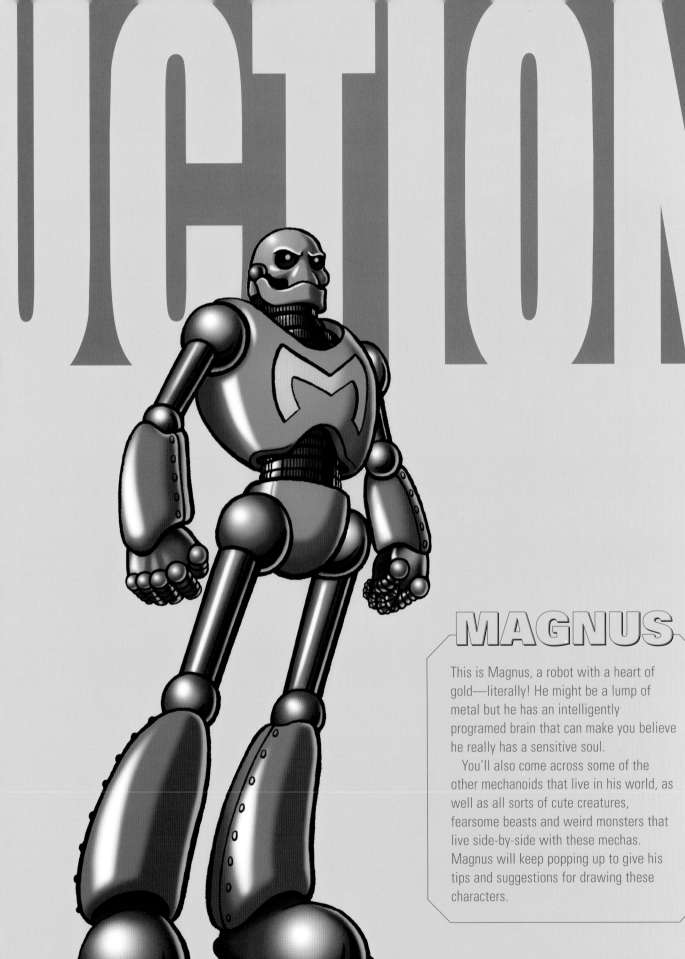

MAGNUS

This is Magnus, a robot with a heart of gold—literally! He might be a lump of metal but he has an intelligently programed brain that can make you believe he really has a sensitive soul.

You'll also come across some of the other mechanoids that live in his world, as well as all sorts of cute creatures, fearsome beasts and weird monsters that live side-by-side with these mechas. Magnus will keep popping up to give his tips and suggestions for drawing these characters.

For the exercises in this book, it will help you to use a hard pencil for sketching light guidelines and a soft pencil for making the final lines of each of your drawings distinct. Hard pencils are number 3 and soft pencils, number 1. They are graded from 1 through 3. Get a number 2 mechanical pencil if at all possible, since this will produce a constant fine line for your final image. If your pencils aren't mechanical, they'll need sharpening regularly.

You'll need an eraser too, since you'll have to sketch a lot of rough lines to get your drawing right and you'll want to get rid of those lines once you have a drawing you're happy with. Keep your eraser as clean as possible.

For adding color, experienced artists have their own preference for certain materials, depending on their drawing style and what they enjoy working with most. The best way to find this out for yourself is to experiment with different materials to see which you like and to learn the different effects they create.

Art materials can be very expensive, but you can get by quite well with just a few of them, so don't be rushed into making unnecessary purchases.

When it comes to coloring, colored pencils are easiest to use. You might want to start with them and then move on to felt-tip pens and watercolor paints when you have developed your skills farther. Cheap photocopier paper was used for most of the artworks in this book, and it's quite adequate for most types of drawing. Only if you're working with paints should you purchase thicker paper since it won't tear or buckle when it gets wet.

In one of the later sections in the book you'll learn about computer coloring—but if you don't have access to a computer, don't worry. You can color your pictures perfectly adequately using other techniques.

CUTE CREATURES

For manga artwork aimed at younger children, cutesy cartoon-style characters are very common and can be an essential element of the plot line and action.

Even in stories aimed at a more mature audience, cute animals often feature as stooges to the main characters, or provide some light relief from the violence of a fight scene.

Whatever kind of creature or character you want to draw, the drawing principles are the same. You start with a set of simple geometric shapes that form the main body masses, then work on smaller details as your drawing skills progress and your confidence grows.

You'll see too how by making a few simple alterations to some cute creatures, they can be changed into evil little characters —so even if cuddly cats and fluffy bunnies aren't your type of thing, it will be useful for you to become proficient at drawing them. You never know what they might develop into.

CUTE CREATURES
CUTE CREATURES
CUTE CREATURES
CUTE CREATURES
CUTE CREATURES
CUTE CREATURES
CUTE CREATURES
CUTE CREATURES
CUTE CREATURES
CUTE CREATURES
CUTE CREATURES
CUTE CREATURES
CUTE CREATURES
CUTE CREATURES
CUTE CREATURES

Cute Cat—Front View

You could probably do a good job of drawing this cute cat just by copying the final picture. But if you learn to construct it one step at a time, this will help you when you are drawing more complicated characters and viewpoints.

Step 1

Take a hard pencil and use light lines to draw an oval for the head. To help you make your picture symmetrical, put a vertical and a horizontal line through the center of it—it's good to get used to drawing lines like this freehand rather than using a ruler. For the eyes, draw two ovals with pointed ends. The ears and long fur around the face can be drawn as rough triangle shapes.

Step 2

Adding a few more simple lines will complete the facial features.

Step 3

Extend the vertical guideline to help you draw the body. Two overlapping circles make its basic shape.

Step 4

The smaller circle will help you draw the slender chest and front legs. The bigger circle will help you position the back legs. The tail sits upright.

Step 5

Add some jagged lines to create the texture of the fur—longer strokes will make a fluffier cat and shorter strokes will make the coat smoother. Add the paws.

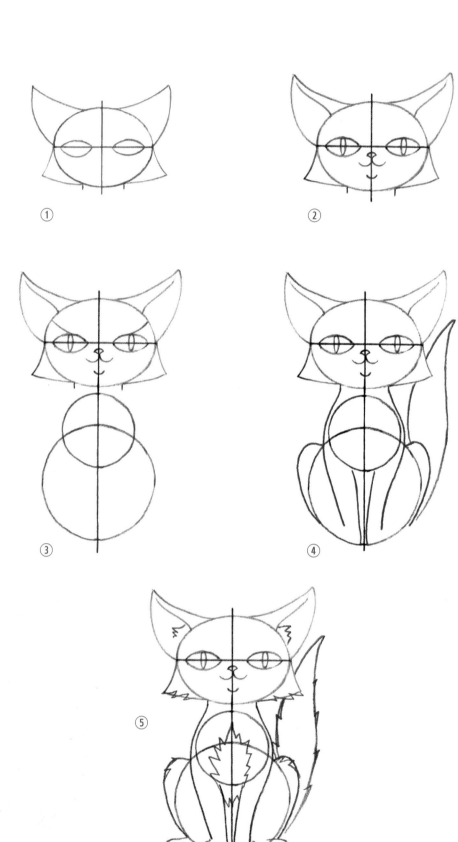

Step 6

Use a soft pencil to make the good lines of your drawing heavier. Erase your rough lines as you go along. Shade in the pupils, but leave a circle of white in the top left of each eye to form the bright highlights that characterize manga artwork. Go over your final lines again with a black felt-tip pen. When the ink is dry, erase any remaining pencil marks.

Step 7

This is what your finished drawing should look like. I've colored mine on a computer—you can find out how to do this later in the book. You might want to color your cat with pencils, paints, or felt-tips instead. Or you can move on to the next exercise and leave the color until later.

Cute Cat—Side View

Here our cute cat has turned his body to the side. His head, however, is turned only half way between the front and side, so it is at a ¾ angle.

Step 1

Draw an oval shape for the head, but make it more squashed than the one you drew for the front view. The change of viewpoint also means that the vertical and horizontal guidelines now curve to follow the rounded shape of the head as shown.

Step 2

Use your guidelines to help you place the facial features as shown. Notice that the eye to the right of your picture is drawn smaller because it is turned farther away. The ear on that side is smaller too.

Step 3

Draw two overlapping circles to help you form the shape of the body. Study the picture to copy the size and positioning of the circles.

Step 4

Add the cat's body outline using your circles to guide you. Make the upright tail long and curved.

Step 5

Add some jagged lines to show the texture of the fur. Shape the paws and add a circle to each eye for the bright highlights—the circle on the eye to the right of your picture will be smaller than the one to the left.

Step 6

Use a soft pencil to go over the lines that you want to form your final drawing—erase your rough lines as you go. Shade the pupils of the eyes black, leaving the bright highlights white. Next go over your drawing again using a black felt-tip pen. When the ink dries, erase any remaining pencil lines, including the framework for the head and the circles that formed the body shape.

Step 7

The great thing about manga creatures is that they can be whatever color you choose—color your cat as you did before or try using a different color scheme.

⑥

⑦

Cute Proportions

In manga, as with all styles of drawing, characters are measured in head heights. This refers to the size of the character's body in relation to its own head. Changing the body's proportions can have a big effect.

The cute cat featured in the previous two exercises is about two-and-a-half heads tall, which is fairly standard for characters of this type. Three heads and two heads tall are also quite common. Remember that the smaller the body is in relation to the head, the younger and cuter the character will look. Study the pictures below to see how I've used different-size circles to change the body shape. Try drawing the cat you drew before but make him shorter or taller.

3 heads tall

$2\frac{1}{2}$ heads tall

2 heads tall

Cat Varieties

Artists can draw many variations of one animal. Here are a few of the different ways that a cat can be interpreted, depending on the style of manga drawing.

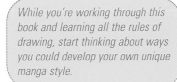

While you're working through this book and learning all the rules of drawing, start thinking about ways you could develop your own unique manga style.

Transformations

If you have a good understanding of how to draw a cute cat, it's easy to work out how you can change its personality—or even turn it into a different animal altogether. The principles are exactly the same— just a few of the details differ.

① This is a ¾ view of our cat, but here I've made him a little more rounded so he looks even cuter.

② Notice how easy it is to turn our cute cat into a fierce enemy. Slanting the eyes and eyebrows and adding some sharp teeth and claws produces dramatic results. An artist can do many other things to convey character and emotion through the features on the face—the cat can be made to look dopey, confused, or excited, for instance—but in most manga scenarios naturalistic animal characters do not normally have a great range of expressions. They simply appear either good or evil.

③ Starting from the same body and head shapes, the cat can be turned into a mouse by changing the shape of the ears and eyes and adding two long front teeth. A long thin tail completes the transformation, but you could also add a chunk of cheese for effect!

④ The same cat can be used to create a pig, squirrel, rabbit, or dog. Try drawing each of them. Turn each one into an evil character too. Look in other books to find pictures of animals and so help enrich your store of ideas when it comes to portraying cute manga creatures or their evil cousins.

④

BEASTS & MONSTERS

Many animals, like deer and rabbits, are only usually found in manga stories as cute characters. Rarely, if ever, are they shown as bad. For ferocious animal characters we have to look in the wild, literally, and to animals that are traditionally associated with violence—lions, and wolves, as well as reptiles like crocodiles and dinosaurs.

Unlike the cute creatures—and certainly unlike humans—these animals are not usually drawn in a particularly stylized way, although there are, of course, some exceptions.

Some manga beasts are created from the features of different animals—this section includes some ideas for inventing such hybrid animals, as well as plenty of examples of creatures that have more than their fair share of wicked-looking teeth and claws.

You wouldn't want a chance meeting with any of these beyond the confines of a zoo. But you're quite safe within these pages. So, sharpen your pencils and try your hand at drawing our selection of beasts and monsters.

Lioness—¾ View

Here is one of the cute cat's relatives—the lioness. Imagine the head as a large ball, with a smaller ball making up the muzzle.

Step 1
Draw two overlapping circles as shown. Draw a curved vertical line on each one to mark the center of the lioness's head. Now roughly sketch in the shape of the eyes, nose, and mouth.

Step 2
Draw on the ears. A few more lines will shape the jawline and neck.

Step 3
Carefully copy the lines I've added to make the lioness more lifelike— notice the creases in the skin above the nose that add to her snarl and the jagged shapes that form the fur.

Step 4
Now for the whiskers, teeth, and tongue. Take some time to get these right since they are crucial to the beast's threatening appearance.

Step 5
Go over all your good lines with a soft pencil so you can clearly see the shape of your final drawing— erase the rough lines as you go. Go over the lines again with a black felt-tip pen. I've used the black pen to shade the nose and mouth area for effect. We'll look at this technique in more detail later.

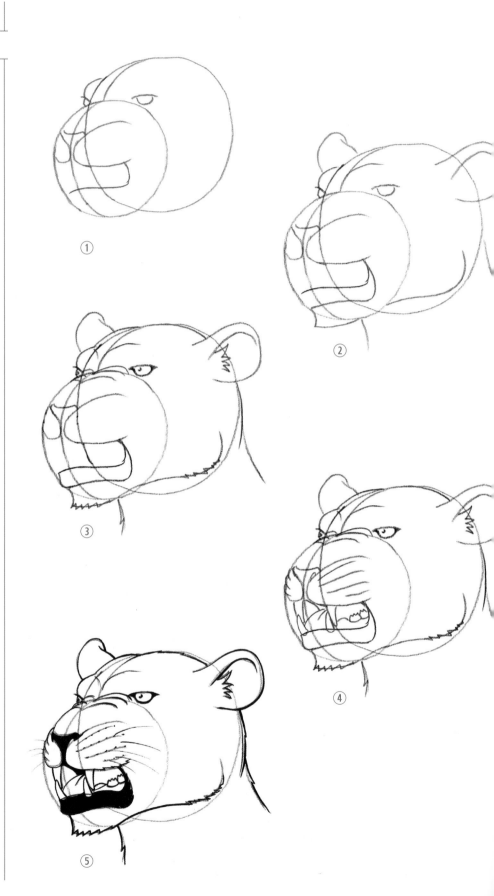

Step 6

Now you can erase the rest of your pencil guidelines, then add some color. Copy the way I've colored the lioness here—notice the different shadows on her face.

⑥

Lion Styles

Although there isn't a great deal of variation in the way larger animal characters are drawn, that doesn't mean they never differ. Here are some ways you could bring a bit of personal style to a creature like a lion while keeping a manga feel—but of course you're free to draw animals in whatever way you want.

① This sculptural style would be appropriate for drawing either a spirit or lion-god. The noble beast is created using lots of sharp lines to give an angular look.

② This is a type of cute cartoon drawing style that can be applied to larger animals to make them look more friendly for younger children. You'll

notice that although there's a very spiky quality to the lines, the lion still looks gentle because of its big, round, glossy eyes.

③ You can soften the ferocity of a wild animal without making it too cutesy—reduce the size of the teeth, round off the sharp edges of the fur, and keep the eyes round.

④ Here smooth strokes have been drawn using a Chinese brush pen, but the eyes and teeth of this beast show that he is far from friendly—small slanted eyes with tiny pupils and some large sharp fangs do the trick. I've also added eyebrows, even though a lion wouldn't really have them. When they're angled down toward the nose, they help to make the lion appear even more fierce.

⑤ These drawings show how the lion is interpreted in traditional Japanese paintings, statues, and puppets. Neither figure looks much like a real lion. The styles have been developed over centuries as one artist copied another but added a little of their own style along the way. These kinds of lions are still used in manga today, especially in fantasy stories or samurai adventures.

⑤

④

Fox—¾ View

One animal that often crops up in Japanese folklore and comics is the fox. Its head is much more angular than that of a lioness.

Step 1

Start with a rough oval shape for the main part of the head, then add a long narrow muzzle. Copy the curves of the vertical and horizontal guidelines. These lines will help you place all the features symmetrically.

Step 2

The ears immediately make your picture identifiable as a fox. The eyes start as two small circles. Outline the nose and mouth too.

Step 3

Keep building up the features of the face. Add the loose fur to the sides of the face. Some simple scribbles form the fur inside the ears.

Step 4

Go over all your good lines in heavy pencil. Add the whiskers and teeth, then go over all your final lines in black ink. A few extra marks will show the texture of the fur around the eyes and at the top of the muzzle. Shade the pupils black, leaving a white circle inside each one. Use solid black on the nose and mouth too.

Step 5

Erase all your pencil marks then add the color. Notice how using white on the eyes adds to the fierceness of the fox's glare.

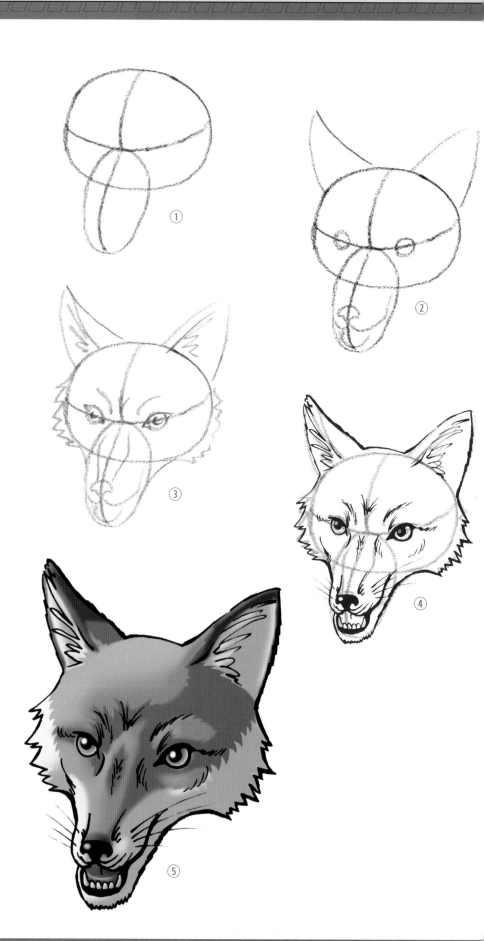

Variations

Once you've mastered drawing a fox, making a few changes to it can develop its character—or turn it into a different beast altogether.

① I've used the same basic framework for this fox, but I've made it look much more evil by slanting the eyes and making the pupils smaller and the teeth longer. I've also used sharper lines for the fur.

② A friendlier fox can be created by making the eyes larger and rounder. I've also made the fur more tufty and used curved lines to make the muzzle less angular. I haven't drawn any teeth, so it appears that they are covered by the tongue.

③ Here's my initial fox sketch, placed next to one of a wolf. You can see that they are really quite similar. To draw the wolf, break it down into the simple steps you followed for the fox, but look at this sketch at each stage to work out what's different—notice that the ears sit farther apart and the eyes are narrower. The muzzle is wider and the snout more pointed. When you've finished, find a photograph of a domestic dog and try drawing it using the same steps. Exaggerate the features to make it look good or evil.

The more you draw animals, the more you'll realize how important it is to look at photographs of real animals to help you capture their features.

Lion Body—Side View

Let's get more ambitious and draw complete animal bodies. We'll start with a fully grown male lion.

Step 1
Start with the head and body shapes, then add the spine and the bones of one front and one hind leg.

Step 2
Add the outline of the flesh around the bones—carefully copy the curves as shown in the picture so you capture the build of the lion's body—notice the lion's puffed-out chest. When you've drawn the line of the belly, add the second hind leg.

Step 3
Work on the rough shape of the muzzle. Add the second foreleg— you can only just see it from this angle. Draw the paws firmly placed on the ground.

Step 4
Add some curves to outline the shape of the face, mane, and tail.

Step 5
Work on the detail of the face and add lots of little curves and curls to the mane to show that the texture is different from the smooth hair on the body. Add a tuft of fur under the chin and on the tip of the tail.

Step 6
Go over your final lines, erasing any earlier mistakes. Ink over the lines in black pen. Add rows of dots for the whiskers and solid black on the nose and mouth.

Step 7

When the ink is dry, erase all your pencil guidelines. If you're not satisfied with the finished result, go back over the steps to see where you went wrong—it may have been the build of the body, the texture of the mane, or the distinctive shape of the eye. When you've figured out which part you really needed to do more work on, try again. Once you've got a drawing you're happy with, add the color.

⑦

Proportion Distortion

You might be surprised to learn that when manga animals aren't supposed to be cute, they are usually drawn with a degree of naturalism, like the lion on the previous pages. Even though the proportions of manga human characters are often highly exaggerated, those of animals seldom are. But some manga artists, influenced by Western comic styles and Hollywood animation, are beginning to give their animals more dynamic characterizations.

① Here's a lion drawn to naturalistic proportions, showing its simplified skeleton and the shape of the head underneath its mane. The lion, as you can see, is long and quite low to the ground. This is because it has to stalk its prey and does not want to be seen above the long grass of the plains.

② Compare this treatment of the same animal. I have enlarged parts of the body and reduced others to emphasize the most powerful parts. The chest is

deeper and the legs more solid, and these changes are made more apparent by slimming down the hindquarters. The head and feet are also enlarged to make room for huge teeth and claws.

In the real world, a lion with these proportions would be at a disadvantage in catching its prey, but in the world of manga, such considerations are unimportant. What matters is that the lion looks impressive and threatening.

③ Now that I've revised the proportions in a rough diagram, I can make a finished drawing of the lion in a suitably ferocious pose. The stance of this new lion is not very different from that of the lion on the preceding pages, but the changes result in a very different-looking drawing with more dynamic proportions, a ¾ angle of view, the head turned, the facial expression, and a display of teeth.

④ With the addition of color, the transformation is complete. In line with the changes to the lion's natural form, I've exaggerated the color.

④

Animal Movement

Animals don't tend to stay still for long, especially in manga, so you need to learn to draw them in all sorts of poses—from sitting, standing, and lying down to stalking, running, and jumping. These pictures show some typical animal poses. I've left the skeleton framework on each body to help you see how the joints can and can't bend.

① These two poses are typical of a lion's behavior. Notice how different the legs look when a lion is sitting down compared with when it's stretching. Although the lion isn't in motion in either picture, the head shows that it's alert, and one of the poses shows that it's ready to pounce.

② There is definitely a sense of movement in each of these drawings. The feet of the cheetah are off the ground and the head is held forward. Each picture suggests imbalance—an impression that if the animals weren't moving forward, they would fall over.

③ Even though these poses aren't balanced, the horse doesn't appear to be moving forward because it has two feet placed firmly on the ground. We still get a sense of the effort it's putting into each stance and the tension in the limbs as the horse lifts itself against the force of gravity.

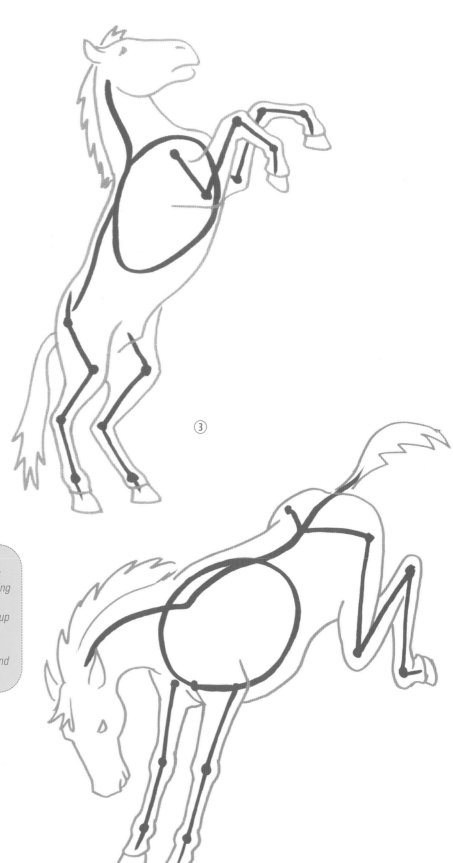

③

The ways animals move are as varied as the species and breeds themselves. When you're watching a movie or TV program featuring animals, watch closely and pick up as much information as you can. You could make some quick sketches of some of the poses and movements you see.

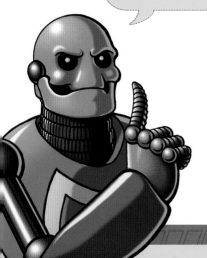

Wolf—Side View

These stages for drawing the body of a wolf from the side also show you how to bring movement into the pose.

Step 1

First draw the main body shapes—the muzzle should be more pointed than that of the lion and the chest takes the form of a large oval lying on its side. All but one of the legs are raised so the bones form zig-zag shapes. The tail is flying up at the back as the animal speeds along.

Step 2

Add the body outline—where you need to create more flesh or muscle, like around the wolf's powerful hind legs, curve the line farther away from the bone.

Step 3

Work on the features of the head—the ear should lie flat, the nose is high in the air, and the mouth is open. Outline the feet and complete the curve of the tail.

Step 4

Lots of little jagged lines around the body outline will help show the texture of the fur. Define the paws and work on the mouth too—the tongue hangs out slightly to show that the wolf is panting.

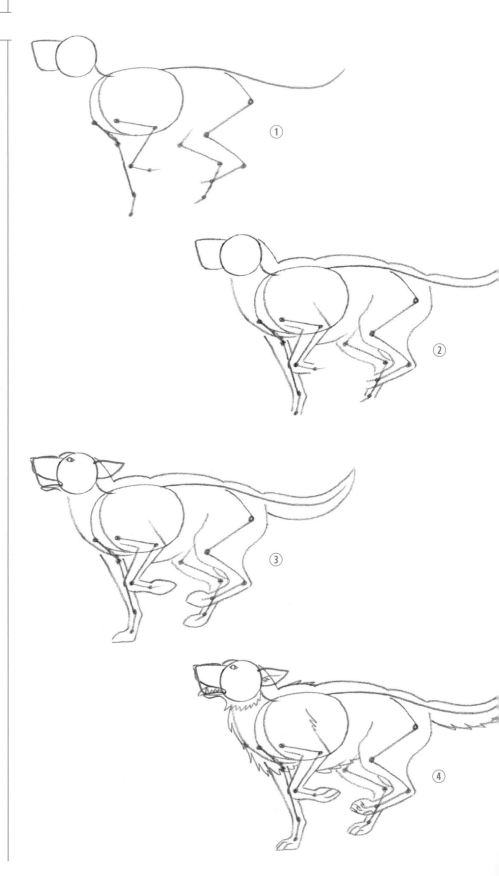

Step 5

Go over your final lines in heavy pencil. Next go over the lines again with a black felt-tip pen, adding some claws to the paws as shown.

Step 6

Erase all the pencil lines that formed the framework for your running wolf, then color him in.

(5)

(6)

Monster Dog

Turn back a few pages and you'll see how I changed a rather ordinary-looking lion into a more ferocious version. You can do this to any creature, and the wolf on the previous page is no exception. This time I'm going to distort the nonthreatening animal even more to create a vicious and demonic monster dog.

①-② Here's a wolflike dog in a jumping pose. By making very slight changes to the skeleton—adding just a little more length to the spine and heightening the neck joint—he can be made to look quite different. The limbs are leaner and closer to the bone, though the outline bulges around the joints to suggest the thickness of the bone endings. The thicker, longer neck works well, as does the slimming down of the stomach area.

This example shows the importance of the skeleton in your drawings: if the skeleton works, then whatever alterations you make to the skin should work too.

③ Before making a finished drawing, I worked out some more details of how I'd like the head to change. I'll strip away all the elements that could look cute: the large, soft ears are reduced to leathery spikes, and the friendly eyes become mere slits and are moved to a higher position on the head. The teeth are an obvious thing to change too. Allowing the fangs to protrude over the lips is a good trick, and a snarling expression always looks effective.

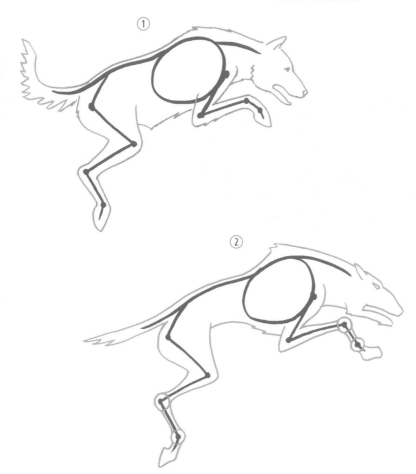

④ I think you'll agree that there's nothing friendly about this beast. Along with the changes to the proportions, I have also drawn the outline of the monster dog with a simplified, angular style. I want to convey a feral creature, ungroomed, half–starved, and hungry for blood. A few lines to suggest ribs and neck sinews are a useful addition.

⑤ This dog is definitely a creature of the night, so I have chosen colors that will blend in with the shadows. In contrast to his body color, the bright mouth and flashing teeth and claws stand out as perilous weapons.

More Skeletons

So far, we have been concentrating on mammals, but there are many more members of the animal kingdom that you might want to draw. Luckily, nearly all animals that live on land have the same parts to their skeletons, even though the proportions may be very different. The human body is also constructed with exactly the same framework as all of these diverse creatures.

① **Frog and crocodile**

The skeletons of a frog and crocodile have the same parts as a mammal's skeleton—each is made up of a head, rib cage, and spine, plus limbs and joints. It's not just the relative sizes of these body parts that distinguishes these creatures from mammals. Their posture is also very different—the limbs are more tightly folded, making the animals more squat.

② **Eagle and crane**

These birds feature heavily in Japanese folklore and have also found their way into many manga stories. With its wings spread, we can see how tiny the eagle's arm bones are in relation to the overall size of the wings. The drawing of the crane shows the way the arm bones bend when its wings are folded against the side of its body.

③ Dinosaur and crow

This dinosaur can stand fairly upright since its strong back legs can bear its weight. Over millions of years, birds have evolved from dinosaurs and still retain some of the same characteristics. The crow also stands on two legs. Its forelimbs are wings, but the overall bone structure is the same. Notice how the proportions of its skeleton differ from the crane's.

④ Wasp and spider

There are exceptions to most rules, as these last two pictures show. Wasps and spiders are invertebrates, so they have no spine. Like all insects, wasps have three main body segments and six legs—the legs are always attached to the middle body segment and the wings have no bones. Spiders have just two main body parts and an extra pair of legs.

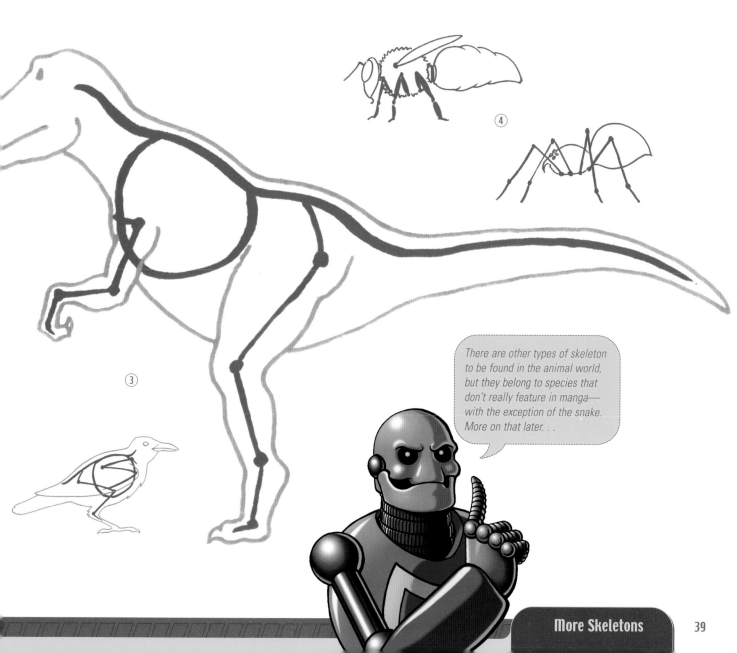

There are other types of skeleton to be found in the animal world, but they belong to species that don't really feature in manga—with the exception of the snake. More on that later. . .

Dinosaur—¾ View

This exercise shows how to draw a dinosaur in action from a ¾ viewpoint. Drawing the body from this angle is a bit trickier but following the steps will help you.

Step 1

A large roughly-drawn circle forms the ribcage. Position and shape the skull, then add a curved line to this to mark the center of the head. Add the parts of the spine and all the bones of the limbs. Once you've completed the skeleton framework, use it to help you outline the flesh of the body.

Step 2

Finish off the forelimbs—the claws are curled under so that they are hidden. When you work on the head, copy the curves above the eyes. The mouth should be wide open, ready for you to add the teeth.

Step 3

Now fill the mouth with jagged teeth. Draw the center crease line of the tongue and draw on the nostrils. Some tiny curves along the dinosaur's back will show the bumps of the spine. Adding crease lines to the body will show the folds of the thick skin. Put some sharp claws on the toes.

Step 4

Go over your good lines with a soft pencil. Then go over these lines again with a black pen.

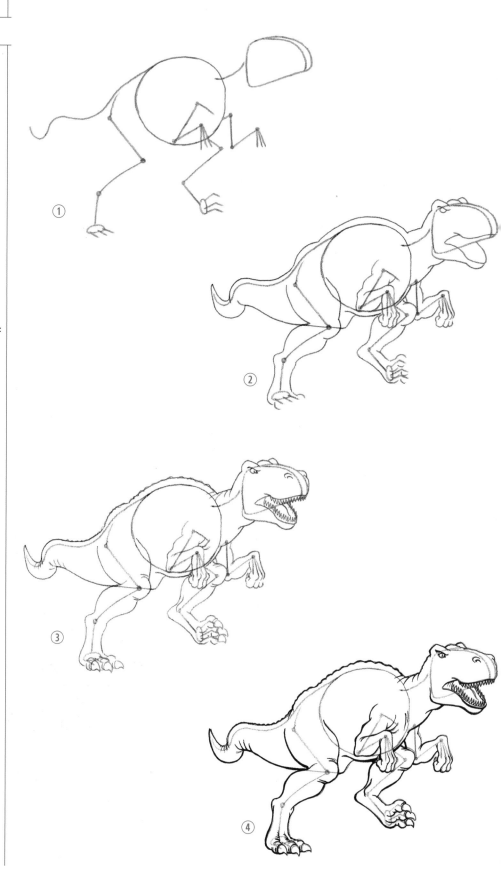

Step 5

Once the pen ink is dry, erase any pencil lines. Now you can add the color—instead of making the dinosaur look naturalistic, I decided to use bold blues and greens. You can choose whatever color scheme you want.

⑤

Creating Hybrids

Several different animals can be combined to create an entirely new species, like the manga dragon we'll draw over the next few pages. Take a look at the finished picture of this dragon on page 45, then study the pictures on this page so you can get an idea of where its different parts derived from.

Lion, snake, and crocodile

The manga dragon has a face similar to that of a traditional Japanese-style lion. Its body and head shape are like a snake's, and its limbs sit like those of a crocodile. But it has features of other animals too—it has the antlers of a deer, the whiskers of a catfish, and the mane of a horse. Its feet are a mixture of human hands and an eagle's claws.

Japanese Dragon

This is a very sophisticated picture, so take your time over each step.

Step 1

Copy the head shape as shown, then add a long curvy tube for the body—overlap the curves of this snake-like shape as if the body is transparent. Later you can erase the lines that make up the sections of the body you wouldn't really be able to see since they lie underneath other sections.

Step 2

Add the bones of the four limbs and copy the frameworks I've drawn for the hands. They are shaped to give the impression that the beast is ready to lash out at any moment.

Step 3

Draw the outline for the flesh around the bones—the lines you drew across the finger bones in the last stage should help you see where the knobby joints are so you can curve your outline around these.

Step 4

Let's leave the body for now and concentrate on the head. First, block in the main shapes—the eyes, nose, jaw, ears, and antlers.

Step 5

Use jagged lines for the fur and teeth. Two curves on the antlers will mark where the skin finishes. Don't forget the tiny pupils and the long curved whiskers.

»

<< Step 6

Add a row of spiky fur along the dragon's spine. Remember that the dragon is twisting and turning, so some parts of its back aren't visible. Draw some long curved guidelines along the body to help you position the ribbed belly in the next stage. Add the sharp claws.

Step 7

As you draw all the lines on the ribbed belly, remember that the belly is rounded, so these lines will curve slightly. Study the picture carefully to work out which way they curve as the body bends in and out—getting this right will add solidity and three-dimensionality to your picture. Add the tip of the tail and attach some fur to the dragon's elbows.

Step 8

Now you should be ready to pick out all the final lines of your drawing and make them heavier by going over them with a soft pencil, then with a black felt-tip pen. If you can easily make out all your good lines, just use a pen. Study the picture carefully to see if there are any lines you missed. Add some extra black to the eyes.

Step 9

When the ink is dry, erase all your pencil lines. Now you can decide on a color scheme. Notice the colors I've used for the fur to make it resemble flames. The inside of the mouth is black to help highlight the ferocious teeth. Don't forget to leave a circle of white on each eye.

More Hybrids

As you get more experienced at drawing animals, you can start to put more of your own ideas into your work. Try creating your own hybrid creatures by mixing the features of different animals. Here are a couple of examples to give you some ideas but if you flip through this book, you'll find lots of skeletons and poses that you could also base your new creations on.

① To come up with this new species, I studied the features and poses of a crane, horse and crocodile, then mixed some of these elements together. Making up mutant animals like this can be great fun. Each new creature can be the starting point for a new manga adventure.

② I created this cute little animal by looking at some pictures I drew in my sketch book a while ago—my new creation has the head shape of a bulldog. A bird's beak takes the place of a nose. The body and pose are similar to a bear's, but the legs are short to help make the character look cute.

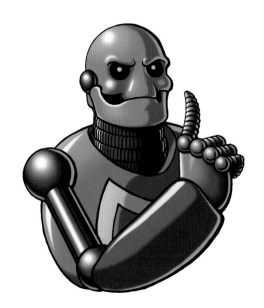

Here are some more animal pictures for you to work from to make up some new manga hybrids of your own. Try changing the proportions of the features you are using. Draw the limbs of one animal in a pose you would usually associate with another creature. Practice drawing different size creatures—some fierce, some cute, some subtle, some weird. Use different viewpoints too.

HUMANOIDS

Hybrid characters that are a mixture of humans and animals are very popular in the most recent comics coming from Japan. All kinds of half-human, half-animal monsters are to be found battling alongside or against favorite manga action heroes and heroines.

We've adopted a similar approach in this next section of the book. You'll also find here a great many robotic characters. Many of these mechas can display all sorts of surprisingly human-like qualities.

Monsters and mechas based on humans are known as humanoids. To create them, you need to know how to construct the heads and bodies of humans, so as a starting point I'll take you through the basic stages of drawing manga males and females.

Once you've mastered drawing the humanoids in this section, you'll have all the skills you need to concoct a tribe of your own fierce and powerful manga beings.

HUMANOIDS
HUMANOIDS
HUMANOIDS
HUMANOIDS
HUMANOIDS
HUMANOIDS
HUMANOIDS
HUMANOIDS
HUMANOIDS
HUMANOIDS
HUMANOIDS
HUMANOIDS
HUMANOIDS
HUMANOIDS
HUMANOIDS
HUMANOIDS
HUMANOIDS

Human Head—Male

This is the head of a teenage manga character, Duke, from a ¾ viewpoint. He's our starting point for exploring humanoids.

Step 1
Copy the shapes that make up the framework of the head. Start with a rough circle and add a vertical guideline to mark the center of the face. The horizontal guideline comes halfway down the whole head shape.

Step 2
From this angle, the iris of the eye on the left of your picture is smaller and more oval-shaped than the one on the right. It also sits closer to the vertical guideline.

Step 3
Work on the facial features and make the jawline more angular.

Step 4
The angular hair falls from a center part, and there is a circular bright highlight on each eye.

Step 5
Go over the good lines of your picture in heavy pencil, then in pen.

Step 6
Once the ink is dry, erase all your pencil lines and add the color. Next try drawing Duke's head from the front and side. Break it down into steps again, thinking how the skull shape and features will alter with a change of viewpoint.

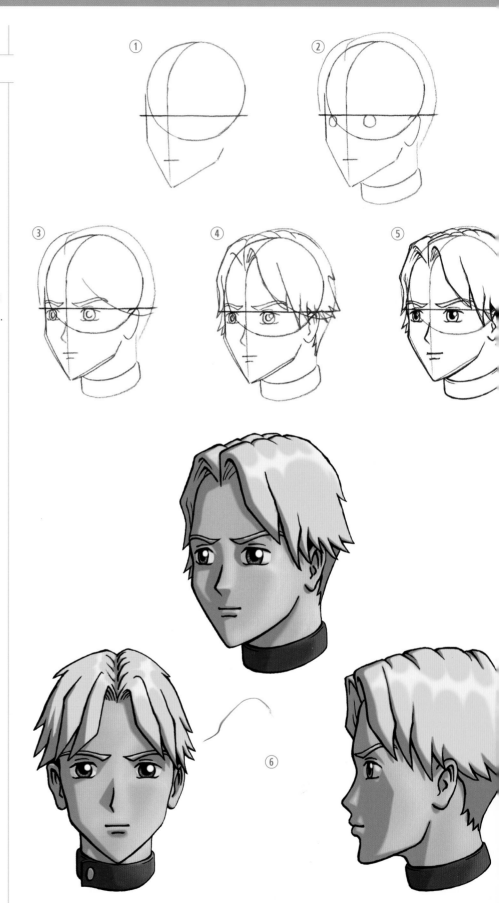

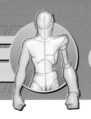
Male Mutations

Once you've practiced drawing a human head, you can alter the features to transform it into whatever mutant you want. Compare each of these pictures with the front view of Duke to see how they differ.

① Ape boy

Short tufty hair, thick eyebrows, protruding cheekbones, dark eyes, and crease lines that show the wrinkled skin all work together to give an ape-like appearance.

② Lion boy

The hair here has been styled to resemble a lion's mane. A rough edge has been added to the jawline to imply fur. Fur has also been added to the ears, which are high up on the head. The eyes point down toward a wide nose and mouth.

③ Lizard boy

The rounded head shape here is accentuated by a lack of hair. The bony spikes on top of the head, the protruding eyeballs, the noseless nostrils, and the thin, wide mouth complete the reptilian look.

④ Bird boy

These large round eyes resemble an owl's. The hair is shaped to look like feathers, and the nose takes the shape of a beak. Notice that eye lashes have been added—these are rare on male human characters.

Human Head—Female

This is the head of a teenage manga girl called Daisy. She is about the same age as the male manga character Duke you learned to draw earlier. Manga girls and women nearly always have much larger eyes than manga males. They often have long, voluminous hair, which is tied back here.

Different angles

The easiest way to draw Daisy's head is from the front. But of course, manga characters are always on the move, so you'll need to be able to draw them from all sorts of different angles. Try copying these different views of Daisy's head— I've added some guidelines to my pictures to help you see how they work three-dimensionally.

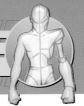

Female Mutations

Taking some of what we've covered in this book so far, we can mix up Daisy's features with those of various animals to make new human hybrids.

① **Bear girl**

Rounded ears that sit high up on the head, a clear hair line around the face and a nose that takes the shape of a snout all give Daisy a bear-like look. Large round eyes and short tufty hair complete the effect.

② **Fish girl**

To create an aquatic look, sweep the hair up into a point, add scales to the ears and draw large round eyes that sit far apart. Notice the distinctive shape of the mouth too.

③ **Monkey girl**

Compare this picture with the ape boy on page 51. The eyes are slightly bigger, as manga girls' eyes tend to be, and the hair longer but still tufty.

④ **Sheep girl**

A matted hairstyle and long curly horns easily identify the animal here. The look is enhanced by sharply angled eyes and eyebrows.

⑤–⑥ **Robot girl**

Most manga robots are human-based too. Here are a couple of different styles based on Daisy's face. See what other variations you can come up with—the great thing about robots is that there's no right or wrong about the way they look!

Perspective

Perspective is the angle and height from which you view an object. If you keep your eyes fixed on one corner of a room and move around, you'll see that the walls, ceiling and floor all converge on this point at different angles according to where you are in the room and whether you are standing up or sitting down. Anything you draw will also be affected by the angle and height of your viewpoint. With the skeleton framework of a human at a ¾ angle, we can see that it looks different depending on our eye level.

① **Mid perspective**

The horizontal red line represents our eye level. Although the skeleton is symmetrical, the other red lines help us to see that all the parts of the body that are above our eye level appear to slope down as they recede (get farther away from us) and those below our eye line slope up. All of these angles converge at a single point on the horizon.

② **High perspective**

Here the horizontal red line shows that the same skeleton is now below our eye level so all parts of the body appear to slope upward as they get farther away from us.

③ **Low perspective**

If we look at the figure so it's above our eye level, all parts of the body appear to slope down to the left.

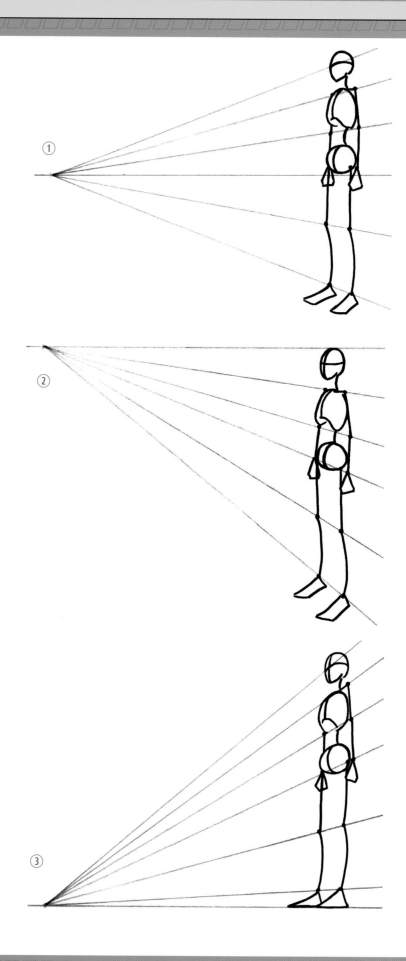

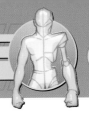

reating Magnus

his is a ¾ view of Magnus the bot with lines added to help you et the perspective right.

Step 1

Draw three oval shapes for the body parts as shown. Add a curved vertical guideline to each body part, then draw a horizontal guideline across the head—the ends curve downward. Copy the angles of the three sloping perspective lines.

Step 2

Add the arm and leg bones—notice that the perspective lines run through the joints.

Step 3

Make the shape of the upper arms and legs by drawing different-size circles connected by parallel lines. Outline the large boots too.

Step 4

Now outline the metalwork of the forearms, hands, and lower legs.
»

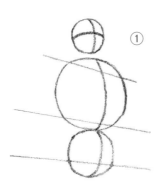

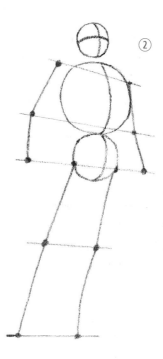

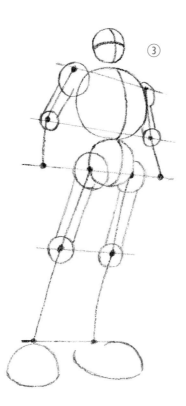

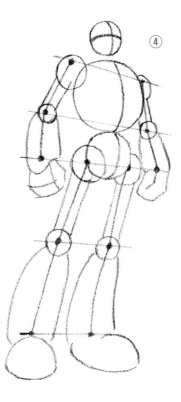

<<

Step 5

Draw on the outline shape of the metal suit surrounding the chest and hips. Work on the main features of the head and add a bit more detail to the lower legs and feet.

Step 6

The rows of horizontal lines down the front of the body create a sub-frame made up of metal disks. Add the letter M to the chest and work on the detail of the giant hands—the thick metal fingers have large circular joints.

Step 7

Pick out all your good lines to form the shape of your final drawing and go over these in heavy pencil. Now go over all your final lines again using a black felt-tip pen. Finally, study the picture carefully to see if you've missed any little details.

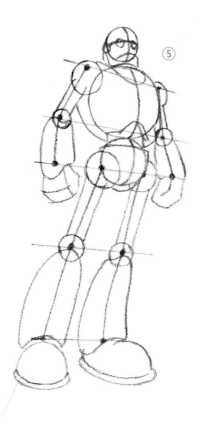

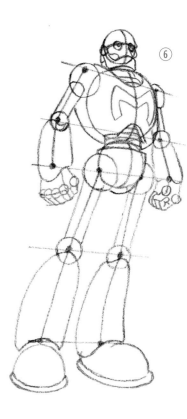

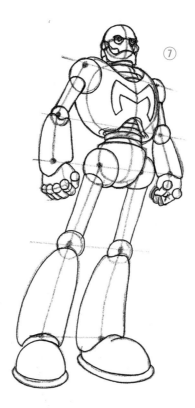

Step 8

When the pen ink dries, erase all the pencil lines that formed your original framework to leave a clean drawing of Magnus. Notice how I've added lots of thin vertical lines to the disks that make up the torso. You can find more information on inking and coloring Magnus later in this book.

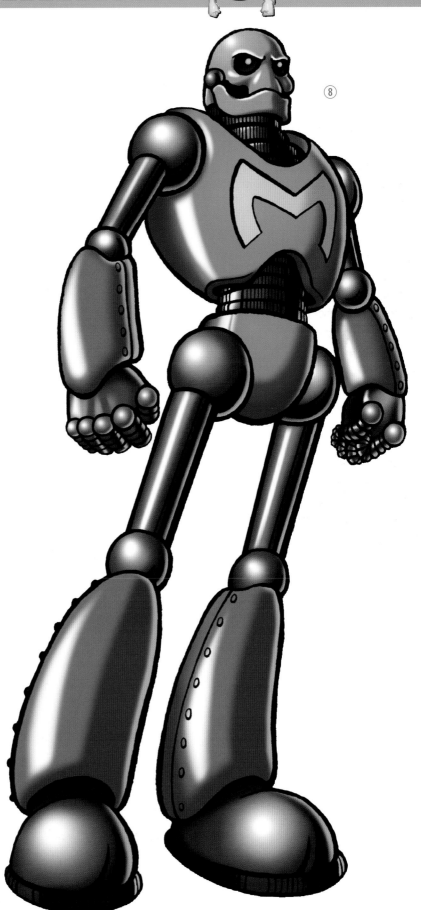

⑧

Centaur

One of the simplest ways of combining human and animal body forms is a straightforward half-and-half split. The top or bottom half of a human is attached to the opposite half of an animal. One creature that takes this form is the centaur, which has featured in stories for thousands of years. It has the torso of a man attached to the body of a horse.

Step 1

Since this figure involves drawing two different species, it's best to concentrate on one creature at a time, so start by drawing the human half as shown. The chest takes the shape of an oval with a chunk cut out to show the edge of the rib cage—the oval is tilted to show that the chest is being thrust forward.

Step 2

Now for the horse—draw a large oval where the man's hips would normally sit to form the horse's rib cage. The man's spine is now also the horse's neck bones. Add the horse's backbone and leg bones—copy the shape of these carefully to capture the centaur's active pose.

Step 3

Start drawing the outline shape of the flesh and muscle around the bone structure as shown. Notice the deep curve of the horse's underbelly and the strong muscles around the upper arms of the human half and the hind legs of the horse.

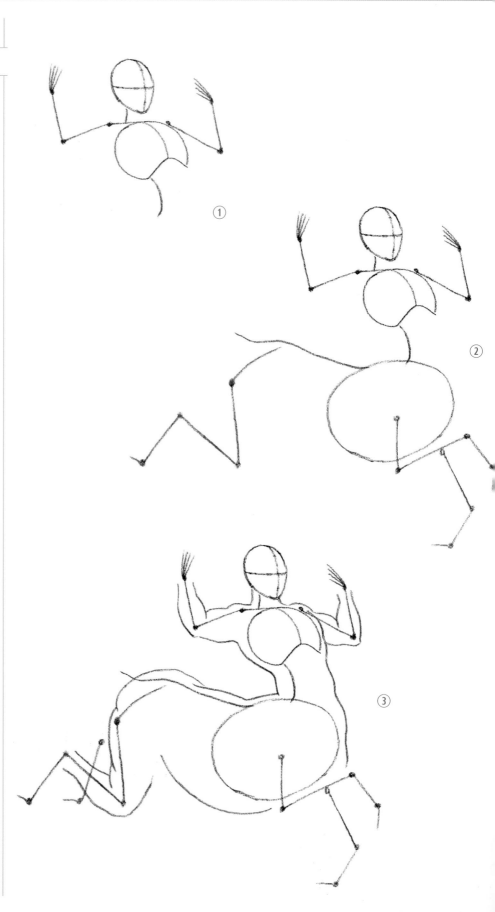

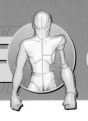

Step 4

Work on the legs and hooves. Notice how the outline curves out around the knobby joints.

Step 5

Place the facial features and work on the shape of the hands. When you draw the sword, make sure it looks as if it has been thrust back, ready for battle. The ponytail on the head should be flying up at the back, just like the horse's tail. Use long, confident pencil strokes to create the curves of these.

≫

④

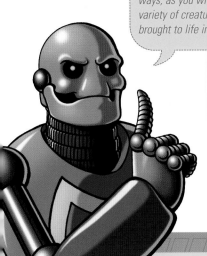

Human and animal forms can be combined in many different ways, as you will see in the variety of creatures that are brought to life in this section.

⑤

Step 6

Add some more detail to the facial features. I've made the centaur's jawline more angular and drawn lots of little lines on the upper body to define the muscle. A few more curves on the body of the horse will add more definition to the muscle and bone here too. Notice the lines on the hair—these help to show the direction in which it is flowing.

Step 7

Pick out the good lines of your sketch and go over them with a soft pencil to produce your final picture. Next go over all your final lines again using a black felt-tip pen. Shade in the eyes, leaving a tiny circle of white on each one.

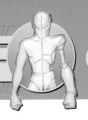

Step 8

Erase all the pencil lines that formed your centaur's skeleton framework, then add the color. I've chosen to give my centaur a zebra's body. I've made his hair black to match his tail.

⑧

Werewolf

The characteristics of a wolf and man are blended together here so that every feature and body part has the flavor of both species.

Step 1

Copy the skeleton framework as shown—the angle of the head and oversized chest is crucial to the beast's overall stance. The short legs make the body appear even heavier.

Step 2

When you add the outline of the flesh, use a high arch to create the hunchback. This will make the head appear to hang even lower.

Step 3

Now work on the head. The ears should be pointed and the eyes small. The beast has a long snout and square jawline. Add two rough triangle shapes to the sides of the face for the fur here.

Step 4

Draw the mouth open to display the teeth. Work on the lines forming the hair, including the bushy eyebrows and chin.

Step 5

Add the hands and feet, including the sharp, curved claws. Copy all the curves that define the chest and stomach muscles. Now use some zig-zag lines along the beast's back and on other parts of the body to show the rough texture of the fur— don't overdo this, since you want the body to retain a human feel too.

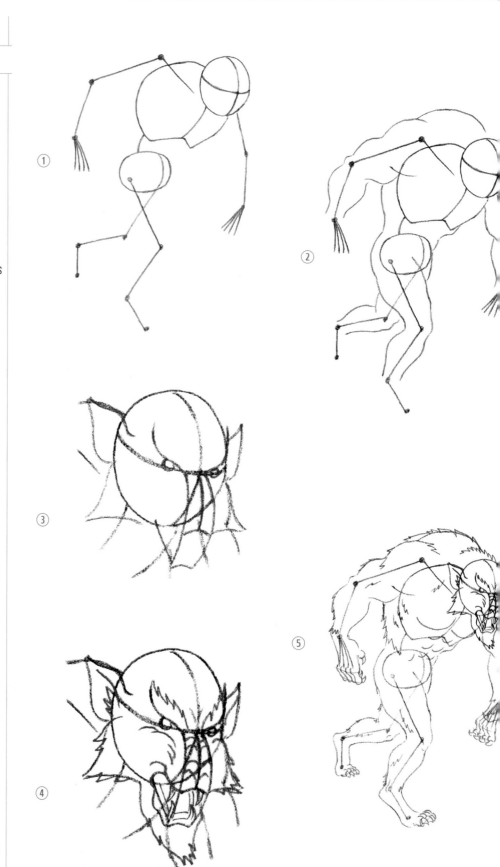

Step 6

Go over all the final lines of your drawing in heavy pencil or go straight to ink if you feel confident enough. When the ink is dry, erase all the pencil marks. Shade around the eyes to make the character look more sinister, then apply the color. Notice how the shadows work to make the beast more imposing. The yellow of the piercing eyes adds to the creature's less than friendly appearance.

⑥

Two-Point Perspective

Knowledge of one-point perspective is all you need for many of the figures you will draw. But if you are tackling a figure that is very solid and blocky, like the robot featured next, it will help you to understand a bit about two-point perspective.

①–③ Simple cube

These diagrams show the effects of perspective on a simple solid cube. You'll notice that the angles recede in two directions. This is two-point perspective. The two points form a horizontal line known as the horizon, or eye line. For the first picture, the eye line is above the cube; for the second picture, it's below the shape; and for the third, it's in the middle.

④ Stacked cubes

If we stack these cubes on top of each other, we have a shape that could form the basis of a three-dimensional figure that is drawn in perspective.

⑤ Robot blocks

This diagram shows the main blocks that make up the body of the robot we will be drawing next. Because the head and chest are at a different angle from the hips and legs, the points at which the angles of the body converge are different. They still meet on the horizon—this is always the case with objects that stand level with the ground.

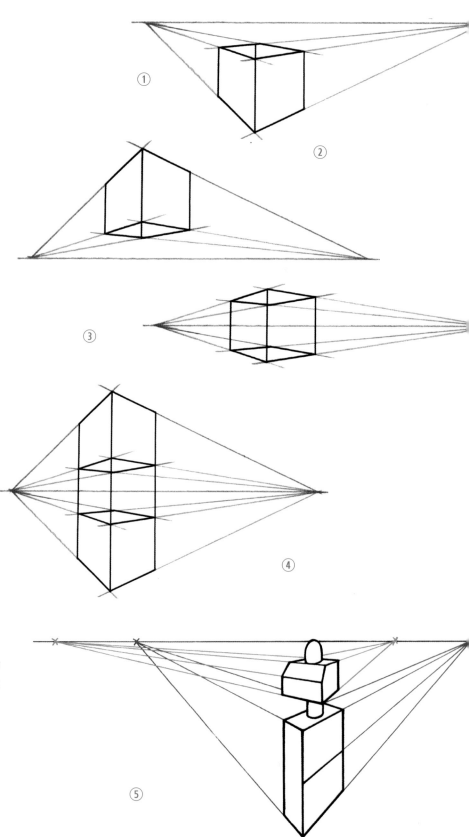

iant Robot

fore you start drawing, take a ok at the finished character on ge 67 so you know what you're ming for.

Step 1

Start with the basic masses that form the head, chest, and hips. Like Magnus the chest is much larger than the head and hips. Notice how the vertical guideline is in a different position on the hips as the figure is twisting.

Step 2

Although this robot doesn't really have bones and joints, drawing them will help you establish the relative lengths and positions of the robotic limbs and work out where they bend. I've added some perspective lines to the lower body to help you draw the legs—the leg to the right of your picture is farther away, so it appears shorter.

Step 3

Turn the chest into a cube and draw a rectangular box around the hips. Use a ruler if it helps. Copy the blocky shape of the upper legs, making the nearest leg thicker. Draw semi circles for knee joints.

Step 4

Add more blocks to form the rough shape of the lower legs and the robot's arms.

>>

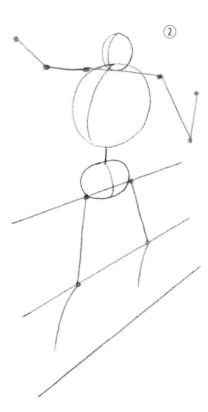

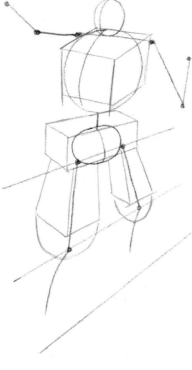

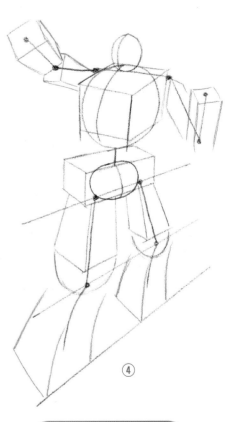

<<

Step 5

Start to refine your robot's shape.
Make the chest more angular, turn
the waist into a narrow, curvy tube,
and add a power pack to the robot's
back. Carefully copy the rest of the
metalwork and make the basic
shapes of the hands—to draw the
giant outstretched hand, start with
the framework for the finger bones,
then map in the palm and the
sockets for the fingers.

Step 6

Add the segmented parts of the
fingers. I've also refined the shape
of the hand to the right of the
picture. Copy all the panels on the
chest and draw the tread on the
soles of the metal feet. I've added a
helicopter to the picture to give the
robot a sense of scale—we can now
see that this robot is about the same
size as a skyscraper.

Step 7

Go over all your good lines in heavy
pencil, then in black felt-tip pen.
Add some more detail to the
helicopter, including the rows of
curved lines that show the spinning
blades.

Step 8

When the ink is dry, erase all your pencil marks. Now you can enjoy adding color. I've added some strips of white to make the metal look like it's reflecting the light. The helicopter is bright green so it stands out against the colors of the robot's body.

⑧

COLOR

At some point, if you haven't done it already, you will want to take your drawings to the next stage and add color to them.

Robotic manga beings like the ones featured in this book are characterized by a smooth metallic sheen, so using color will really bring out their features. The realistic look of their metalwork can also be greatly enhanced by accurately applying shading. I'll show you the basic technique, but to get really first-class results you do need a lot of experience, so don't worry if you can't replicate the finish of my drawings.

Most manga artwork created today is colored on a computer. I'll take you through the stages of doing this, and show you how to create similar effects using felt-tip pens. Coloring by computer gives a very smooth finish, but you can have just as much fun with pens and pencils.

I'll also show you how to use white ink to give your pictures a slick outline and to add a few finishing touches.

Building up color needs planning and takes a bit of practice—a good drawing can be easily spoiled at this stage of creation. It's worth taking some photocopies of your line drawings and coloring those rather than your originals, just in case you make mistakes. Don't worry if you don't get things right first time. Becoming a good manga artist doesn't happen overnight— so keep practicing.

COLOR
COLOR
COLOR
COLOR
COLOR
COLOR
COLOR
COLOR
COLOR
COLOR
COLOR
COLOR
COLOR
COLOR
COLOR
COLOR
COLOR
COLOR
COLOR
COLOR

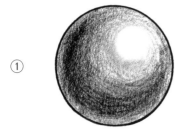

①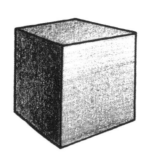

②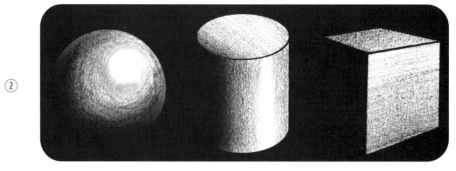

Light & Shade

To use color effectively, you need to understand how light and shade affect an object.

① Daytime shadows

The shapes shown here form the basis of most objects. Light is hitting them from an upper-right direction. The surfaces facing toward the light will therefore appear brighter than the parts that face away. The parts facing away will not be completely black, however, because light also bounces off walls, floors and other objects to faintly illuminate these areas.

② Night-time shadows

At night, when objects are lit directly from artificial light sources, there may be no light reflecting off other things to help illuminate the parts of an object that face away from the light source, so these areas can merge into the darkness.

③ Simple shading

First decide on the direction the light is coming from, then lightly shade the surfaces of your picture that aren't facing the light directly. In my picture, the light is coming from top right again. I've used a very soft pencil, holding it at an angle but without pushing down too heavily.

④ Creating shadows

Some parts of a complicated object like this robot will block out the light from other parts—an arm might cast a shadow on a leg, for instance. Keeping the light direction in mind, imagine where various body parts might cast shadows on other parts and shade those areas darker.

⑤ Hidden areas

Some parts of the robot are tucked away, like the little crevasses under close-fitting joints. Shade these parts more heavily.

⑥ Angles

Polish your picture by working across each body part and imagining the subtle ways that light falls on it. Shade the parts to different degrees, depending on the angle of each part in relation to the direction of light.

⑦ Adding backgrounds

Here is my finished picture against two different backgrounds. A gray background makes the lighter areas stand out more and helps show the effects of reflected light around the left and lower edges of the body parts. I've also put the same drawing on a black background and removed the reflected light. Now you can see that it blends in with the background completely. This effect is often used in manga to create atmosphere.

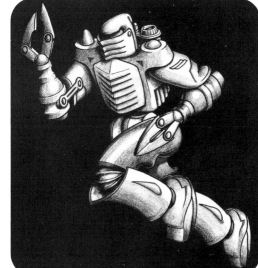

Inking

Manga artwork is usually characterized by slick outlines and smooth shading and coloring. Using the drawing of Magnus that we created step-by-step on pages 55–57, I'll show you some simple tricks to bring him up to manga standard.

① Black outline

This is the basic drawing of Magnus outlined with a thin black pen. It's not bad, but it could be made to look a lot stronger without much more work.

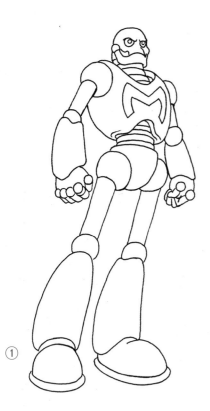

② Adding ink

Thickening the whole outline makes Magnus look much bolder and more solid. I've varied the width of the lines too—they're thicker along the right-hand side of each body part and on the underneath edges, which helps to suggest that these parts are facing away from the light source. For this, you could use real artist's pens with flexible points for dipping into ink, but these are difficult to use and the same effects can be achieved with a thicker felt-tip pen. I've also added some lines to the fingers to show the metal grooves and filled a few areas with solid black, like the corners of the mouth and the underside parts of the robot's metal jacket.

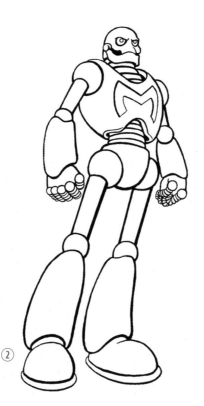

③ Line shading

The same pens can be used to add some metallic effects to the body work. I've shaded the robot's cylindrical body using lots of little vertical lines. I've also added some small circles to the arms and legs to make the rivets that fasten the pieces of metal together.

Coloring

These days, most manga artwork is colored digitally by computer, but not everyone has access to computers and expensive graphics packages. Here I'm using artist's quality marker pens to color Magnus, but you can get similar effects with ordinary felt-tip pens.

① **Robot color swatches**
Magnus is really only five colors: gray, blue, green, yellow, and gold. To show how light falls on him (from top left), we also need to use darker shades of each of these colors, so you'll need felt-tip pens in the different shades you can see here.

② **Adding the color**
First use your darker shades—the colors you need are shown next to the picture. Apply them to the areas facing away from the light and to areas that are in the shadow of other parts of the body.

③ **Larger areas**
Now you can color the bigger areas using lighter colors—when you do this, leave some strips of white. This will have the effect of making the surfaces look shiny.

④ **Smaller parts**
Continue to add color using the swatches next to the picture to guide you—notice how I've used different grays to enhance the shine patterns on the metalwork.

⑤ **Final color**
Once you've finished with your felt-tip pens, you can clean up your picture with the help of a bottle of white ink and a fine brush. Use these to blot out color around the edges of your picture where the color has bled over the lines. They are also good for adding highlights and sparkle to the metalwork. I've used them to help me add a glow of reflected light to the right-hand side of the picture—I drew thin strips of white on the head, chest, and arm, let this ink dry, then colored these strips light blue.

①

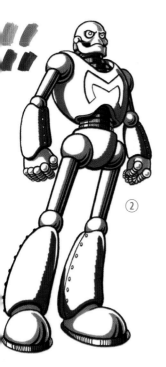

②

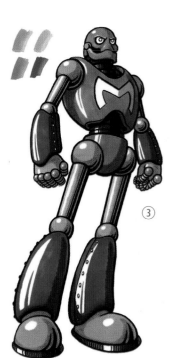

③

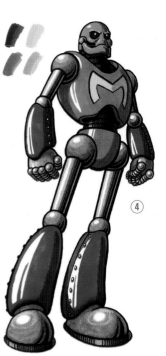

④

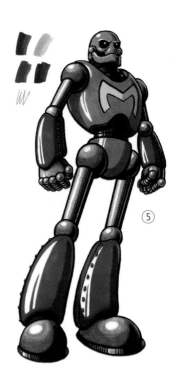

⑤

Cyborg Girl

Cyborgs are usually the result of a horrific accident or battle where a human character has been injured and has had to have surgery to replace real body parts with mechanical elements. This usually turns them into powerful bionic beings. This cyborg girl has retained a very human shape, apart from the flame-throwing weapon that replaces her left arm.

Step 1

Draw the basic shapes for the head, chest, and hips as if you were sketching a human character. Add the sections of the spine and the limb bones—the bottom section of the mechanical arm is much longer than an ordinary forearm would be.

Step 2

Draw the curves of the flesh and muscle around your skeleton framework. The figure has strong, rounded muscles that are much more defined than those of most nonbionic manga females.

Step 3

Draw some lines to form the basic shape of the flame thrower. Add the outline for the hands and feet, then start to work on the facial features and hair.

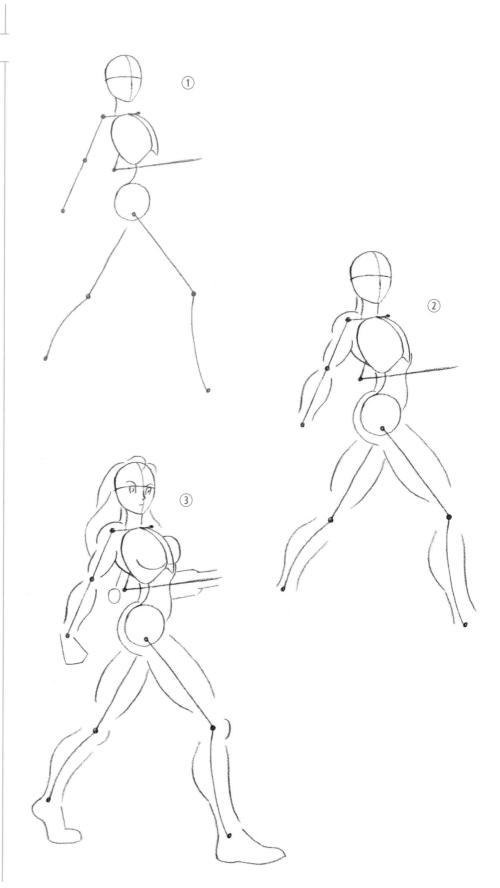

Step 4

Work on all the metalwork that surrounds the cyborg's feminine body as shown. Add the protective armor to the head and finish the lines forming the shape of the mechanical arm.

Step 5

Fill in more of the detail on the metal suit like the ribbed sections that allow the knees to bend. Add the long curved blade to the end of the good arm and shape the fist. A few little curves at the end of the barrel of the flame thrower will create the impression of smoke.

Step 6

Go over all the final lines of your drawing with a soft pencil, including all the detail, so you can clearly make out your final picture.

>>

<<
Step 7

Spend some time carefully going over all your heavy pencil lines with a black felt-tip pen. There's a lot of detail, so it's best to use a very fine point. When the ink is dry, erase all the remaining pencil marks.

Step 8

Next go over some of the lines again using a pen with a slightly wider point to vary the thickness of your outline. This cyborg has an extremely slick look, so your line work should be smooth and graceful. Fill some areas with the black as shown to make the figure look more solid.

Step 9

You'll notice that the metallic effects are much more complicated than those we saw when drawing Magnus. This is because our cyborg girl has ample curves and not simple cylinders and spheres. As with any metallic object with various surfaces, the light will catch it in many different ways, and so create all sorts of visual interest.

On the next four pages you'll learn how to create these effects digitally. If you don't have a computer, don't worry. You can achieve a very good result using felt-tip pens. Any mistakes you make while coloring can be corrected afterward with the help of some white drawing ink and a fine brush.

The next time you pass a highly polished car or motorcycle in the street, study the shadows and reflections on the chrome and other metallic surfaces. This will help you create these same effects on robotic characters you draw in the future.

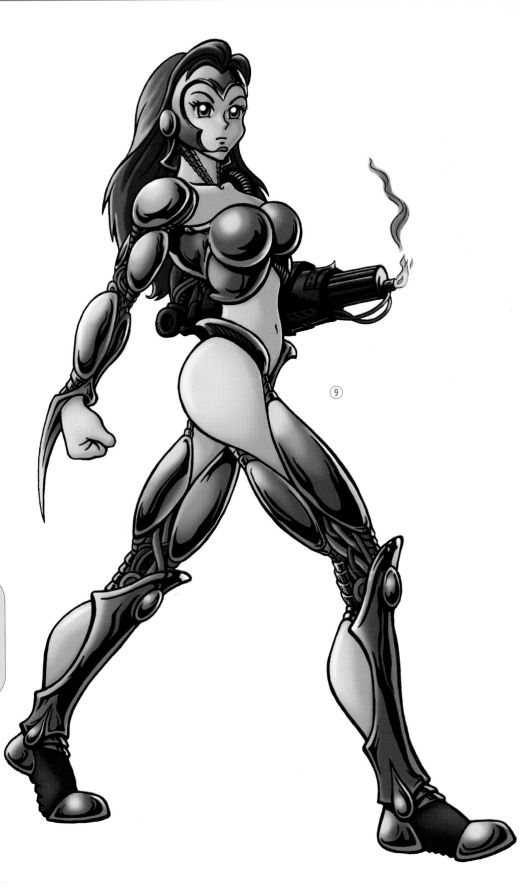

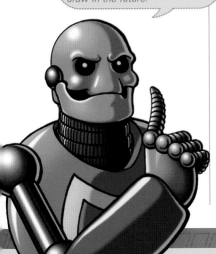

Computer Coloring

Most manga artists color their artwork by computer these days. The programs and techniques can take a while to learn, although the principles involved are very similar in the various coloring programs. For the following exercise, I used Adobe Photoshop, one of the most popular and widely available programs. When you color by computer, remember always to save your work after every stage.

Scanning and preparation

First, the line drawing that you want to computer-color must be converted into a digital file for the computer. It's always best to scan your picture at a high resolution—say, 500 dpi—and as a gray-scale image to ensure that you get crisp lines. When you open the image in Photoshop, reduce the resolution to 300 dpi, which is about the maximum you'll ever need to print with. A higher resolution will only slow down your computer. The next stage is to convert the image (in Image>Mode>) to RGB, which allows you to start using color.

At this point it's a good idea to look at your work close up and in detail. If you see blotches, clean them up. You can usually get away with leaving small blemishes, so don't worry about cleaning every tiny imperfection. No one will notice them, and your time is better spent assessing the overall look of your work. Use the Eraser tool for cleanup.

The final preparation stage is to make sure your background color is white. Choose Select All (Apple + A) and then New Layer Via Cut (Apple + Shift + J). Set the Blending Mode of this layer to

Multiply, name it Line Art, and then Lock it. You shouldn't need to touch your original artwork again.

Hint: I use a Mac computer, on which the command key is labeled with an apple symbol. If you have a Windows-based computer, use the control key, labeled ctrl, for the same function.

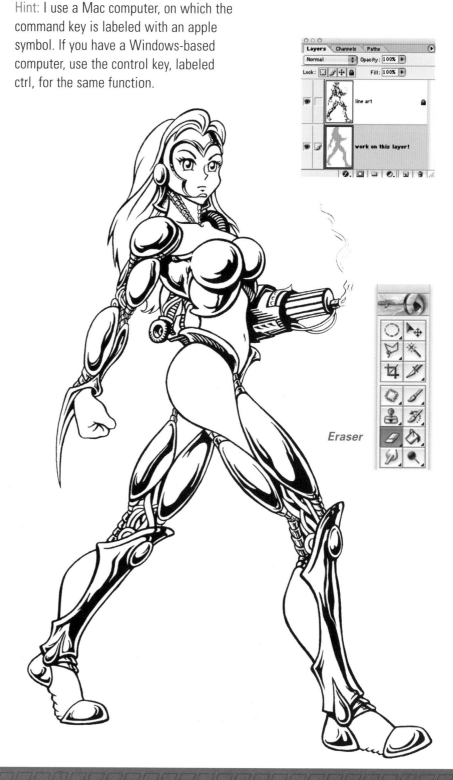

Eraser

① First color

You will apply the color (called Flat Color) on the layer below that of your original line artwork. Start with the color that makes up the biggest area of your figure—here it's our cyborg girl's armor, and I'm using a light gray for it. You need to apply this color to your whole figure to separate it from the background. You'll change different areas to other colors in a bit. To apply the gray, magnify your image, then use the Polygon Lasso tool to select the area. Now fill it up using the Bucket tool.

② More colors

Now you need to change part of your figure to the color that makes up the next-largest area of your figure— here it's our cyborg girl's skin color. Use the Polygon Lasso tool again, then fill the area using the Bucket. Or change the color using Image > Adjustments > Hue/Saturation (Apple + U). Repeat this process, selecting smaller and smaller areas each time. Hint: When you do this, you only need to concentrate on drawing a Selection line between areas that are at present the same color. Once you've drawn your rough selection area, you can use the Magic Wand with the Alt key pressed to deselect any areas that you included accidentally.

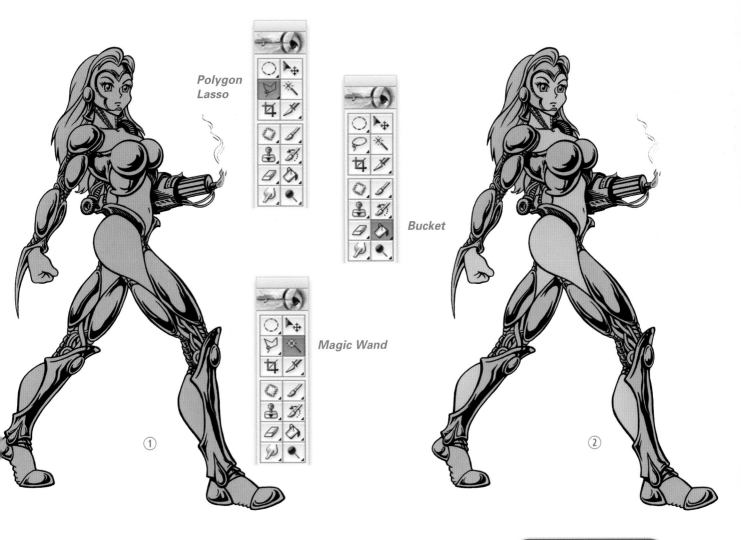

Polygon Lasso

Bucket

Magic Wand

① ②

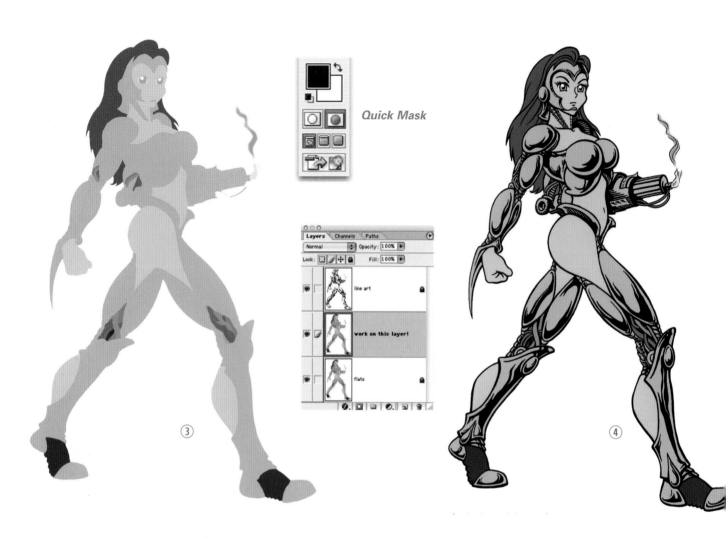

Quick Mask

③ Saving the flat color

Once you've laid all the flat color down, select New Layer Via Copy to copy the layer. Name the new copy of the layer (which will appear at the bottom) Flat Color, then Lock it. You shouldn't need to change this layer again until you clean up with the Magic Wand tool later on. You should have been saving your work regularly, but save now if you haven't already.

We'll only work on the layer in the middle from now on. Picture 3 shows the same stage without the outline.

④ Adding shadows

Now it's time to add some shadows. For this, we'll be using Quick Mask. Click on the Quick Mask icon or press Q. Using the Brush tool, paint an area you want to be in shadow. Don't worry about going over the lines— we'll fix them shortly.

Hint: To make Quick Mask easier to use, double-click on the icon in the Tool palette to view its Options palette. Check Color Indicates: Selected Area and choose a dark mask color. To see what you've just

done, leave Quick Mask mode (press Q again or the icon in the Tool palette). If you want a more feathered look for the area of the image you've selected, use a softer brush.

Now you can clean up the selection by going to your Flat Color layer and using Alt plus the Magic Wand tool as you did in step 3, above. Go back to your working layer (the middle one) and use Image >Adjustments >Hue/Saturation to shade to your taste, or just fill it up with the Bucket tool.

⑤ **Highlights**

The same technique you used for the shading can be employed to make well-defined areas of light and dark. This is how I gave our cyborg girl's armor that chrome look.

Hint: If you would like exact control over the area of highlight, you can magnify the image and use the Lasso tool to select the shapes you want. For most of the images in this book, I used the Dodge tool, which softly lightens colors wherever it is applied. If you prefer a more painterly style of shading, you can use it and the Magic Wand to mask off the areas you're working on.

Your work is now ready to print out.

Dodge

⑤

PROJECTS

To end this book, we're going to embark on a project that involves creating an alien character, from the very first ideas to the finished color artwork.

Manga stories that are set in the future or outer space are usually populated by weird and unearthly beings like this one, as well as fantastically complex vehicles, robots, and weaponry.

Inventing alien characters—and drawing them—isn't as hard as you might think, although there's no definitive route to doing it. Each individual creature will evolve differently depending on the artist's imagination, experiences, and drawing style.

But the great thing about these characters is that there are no real rules like the ones that apply to drawing human beings. Alien bodies can behave in any way you want them to and have any range of unusual qualities.

Once you've mastered how to draw the alien featured on the following pages, you should be well equipped to release all sorts of alien beings of your own into the manga world.

PROJECTS
PROJECTS
PROJECTS
PROJECTS
PROJECTS
PROJECTS
PROJECTS
PROJECTS
PROJECTS
PROJECTS
PROJECTS
PROJECTS
PROJECTS
PROJECTS
PROJECTS
PROJECTS
PROJECTS

Creating an Alien

There's no parcticular route to creating new characters. Each character evolves in its own way through many stages of drawing—especially if your principals come from other planets. When you aren't sure what you want to draw, there's nothing more daunting than a blank sheet of paper.

① Doodling

A good way to get started is to give yourself a problem to solve. Take a pencil and some scrap paper and lightly draw a squiggle.

② Imagining

Looking at your squiggle from different angles, try to make out a face or body hidden among the lines. Draw directly onto your squiggle to develop what you see. This squiggle made me think of a bird-like form.

③ Shaping ideas

After repeating this process several times, I start to get inspiration for the kind of alien I want to create, and see insect and crablike qualities that might work well for an alien creature.

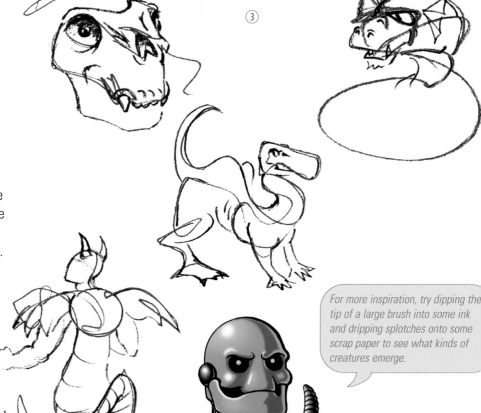

For more inspiration, try dipping the tip of a large brush into some ink and dripping splotches onto some scrap paper to see what kinds of creatures emerge.

Seeking Inspiration

Having arrived at the kind of look I want to achieve, I turn to my sketch books for further inspiration. All the examples shown were done during a trip to a natural history museum, and provide good reference for my alien project. Incorporating features based on the natural world can help to make your creatures look believable.

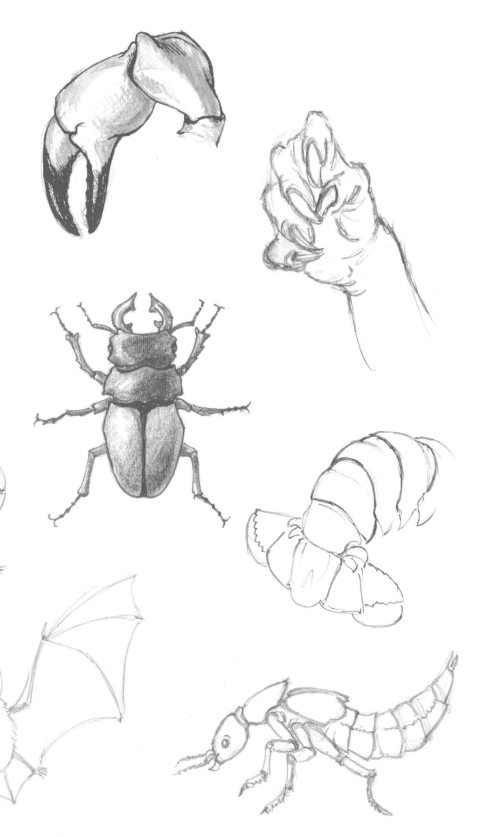

Sketching the Alien

Working from my rough doodles and sketch books, I start to develop some alien life forms. Gradually a character starts to evolve, and each picture takes me one step closer to creating a character I'm happy with. I want my alien to be fearsome yet graceful and appealing.

If you visit a natural history museum, take a sketch book with you to draw any animal features that appeal to you. Look at pictures in wildlife books or on the Internet too.

Developing the Alien

① **Color sketch**

Roughly adding some color to my favorite design helps me to visualize how a finished version might look. It's almost there, but I feel it could still be made to look more scary and other-worldly.

② **The pose**

For a start, it needs a more dynamic pose. Drawing the skeleton framework of a human allows me to see if a pose will work.

③ **Design changes**

During the process of sketching my alien in its new pose, I continue to develop its body features.

④ **The final sketch**

Producing a final sketch, I further refine the details and proportions. I could continue to change elements, but at some point you have to settle on a final design. I'm now ready to ink and color my final picture, but in the next few pages I've broken it down into steps so you can copy it.

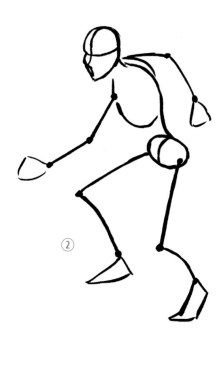

①

②

③

④

Drawing the Alien

Here are the steps to making a precise drawing of the final alien character I came up with on the previous page.

Step 1

Although this alien's overall body shape is quite human in form, there are some vital differences in the make up of its skeleton. The outline for the head is triangular, and I've put an extra joint in the neck to make this longer and more mobile. Notice the dramatic arch of the spine too. The chest oval is much larger than the oval for the hips.

Step 2

Place the arm bones and joints as shown. For clarity, one arm is drawn as if it isn't connected to the body. Notice how the legs differ from a human's. The section between the knee and ankle is short and the ankles sit high up, more like those of many animals.

Step 3

Add the main parts of the body outline as shown—the body is made up of lots of separate segments.

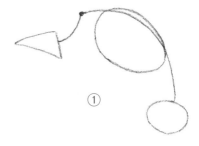

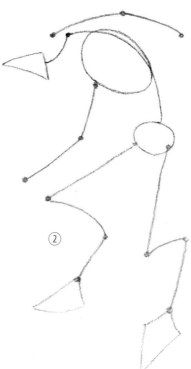

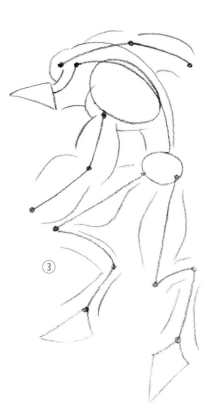

Step 4

Fill in the gaps of your alien's body outline—if you turn the page, you'll see a picture of the finished beast, which will help you work out what body parts all the different lines belong to. Work on the shape of the head too. The hands resemble a human's, while the feet are more like an animal's hooves.

Step 5

Build up the definition of the features gradually—here I've drawn in the flesh of the fingers and worked on the shape around the hips and limb joints.

Step 6

Now for some of the more lethal parts, like the giant fangs and claws. Add the sharp blade of the weapon too. Work on all the segments running down the neck of the spine and the plates that form a shell to protect the creature's back.
»

Step 7

Work on the rest of the detail, like the features of the snarling mouth and the jagged spines on the legs. Add some little lines to show the protruding ribs and draw the curves that show the muscles on the tiny stomach. Notice the extra lines that show the fleshy parts of the hand.

Step 8

Use a soft pencil to go over all the good lines of your drawing so you can easily make these out.

Step 9

Ink over all your heavy pencil lines using a black felt-tip pen. When the ink is dry, erase all the remaining pencil marks, especially the lines forming the skeleton framework.

Step 10

Now add color to your picture—this is what it will look like if you color it digitally. After coloring, you could have some fun thinking about what kind of creature this beast might be attacking—once you've come up with a design for the enemy creature, put the two beasts together in one picture.

⑩

Designing a Robot

Just as manga artists use the features of animals and humans to create mutant creatures, all sorts of everyday objects can provide inspiration for drawing robots.

Here are some of the objects I found lying around my home. They are all quite ordinary things, but any of their features or geometric qualities could be incorporated into the design of a new robot character.

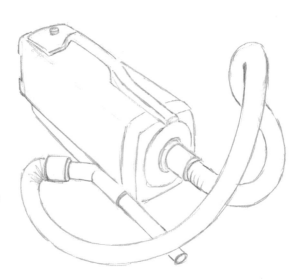

vacuum cleaner

computer mouse

electric whisk

binoculars

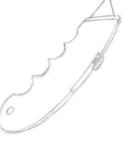

box cutter

soap dispenser

pliers

hairdryer

kettle

perfume bottle

watering can

Junk Robot

Here are all the household objects assembled into a very rough robotic form. I've used some objects more directly than others and also changed their relative sizes—notice, for instance, the giant binoculars that form the power pack on the back. This design still needs a lot of work—the last thing a manga super mecha wants is to look as if he's made from giant kettles and vacuum cleaner parts. Before you turn this page and find out how I develop him further, try the following exercise.

Exercise

Find some objects that interest you around your home or pictures of objects in books. They might be airplane parts, engines, tools, electronic items, or anything else that could be made to look robotic. Build up a few pages of small sketches of these items, then try using all or part of each object to assemble a robot of your own. Developing new characters is a lot of fun, but it can also be a lengthy and involved process.

MANGA
MECHAS AND MONSTERS

Developing the Robot

To bring our collection of junk to life requires a few more stages of development.

Step 1
I've chosen a chunky human form for my robot.

Step 2
Because the physique I've decided on is very bulky, my robot could easily look cumbersome, so I've gone for a dynamic pose.

Step 3
A mechanical version of my running human is now easy to draw.

Step 4
Next I built up my robot part by part, basing the design on my sketch of a junk robot from the previous page. This time, however, I only used the household objects as an inspiration and instead invented new parts to suit my machine. Deciding on the final shape of these parts can involve a lot of redrawing, but going over your final lines in heavy pencil and erasing all the mistakes will make your final design much clearer.

Step 5
To farther disguise my source material and to give more of a manga feel, I've added some extra details like the slatted metal visor and chest panel. When you're happy with your robot, go over it in black pen. Once the ink is dry, erase all remaining pencil marks.

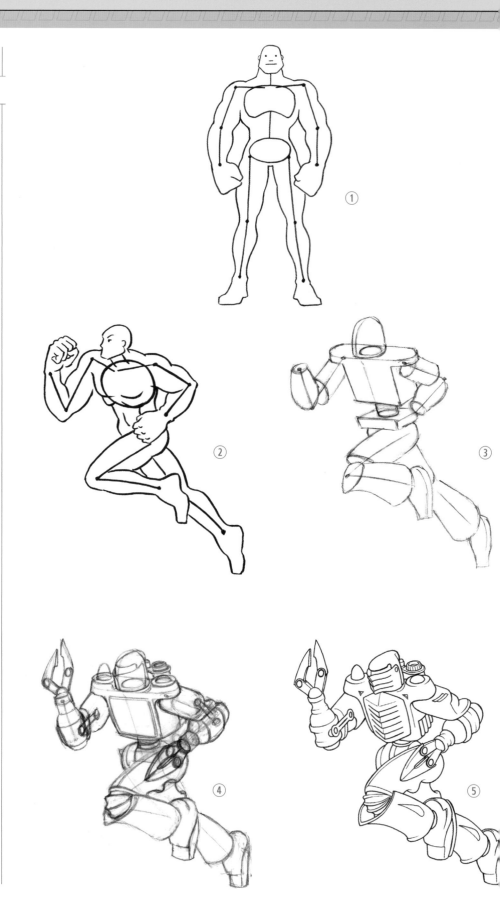

Step 6

Before coloring your own robot, you might like to flick back to pages 70–71 to see how you might approach shading and so give him the appearance of solidity.

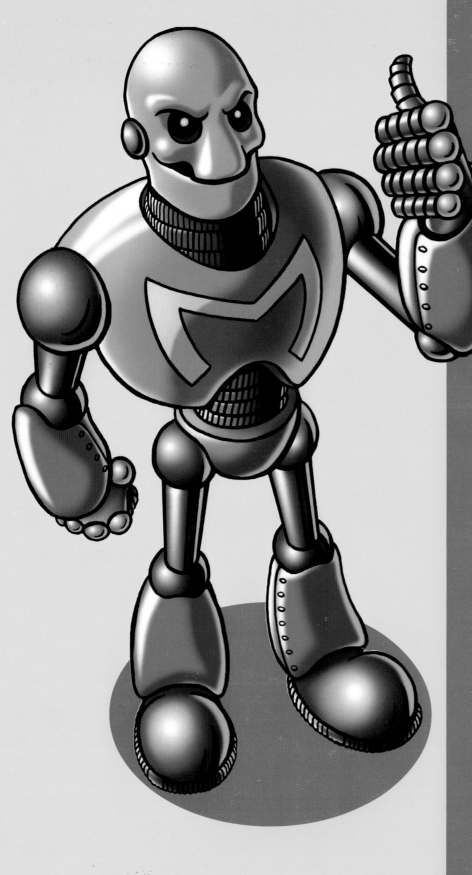

I hope you've enjoyed creating the weird and wonderful bunch of creatures that appear in this book. Remember that any sketches you make of objects or animals in the world around you could come in handy for drawing monsters and mutants, so keep a sketch pad with you at all times—you never know when a casual look through it might give you the inspiration you need.

Other books in this series will show you how to create a variety of male and female human characters that you might want to draw fighting against or alongside the animals, monsters, and mechas found here.

You'll also find information on drawing backgrounds and putting figures together to create dramatic scenes. You can find out how to build up these scenes to create a comic-strip story too.

So keep exploring the world of manga—and, most important of all, keep drawing!